FOCUS

For every child who
dares to try,
Your focus will help
you reach the sky.

Milo and Emma loved to play, But when class began, their minds would stray.

Their teacher smiled and softly said,
"Focus gives strength to heart and head."

FOCUS

Milo tried first
with puzzle in view,
So many pieces!

What could he do?

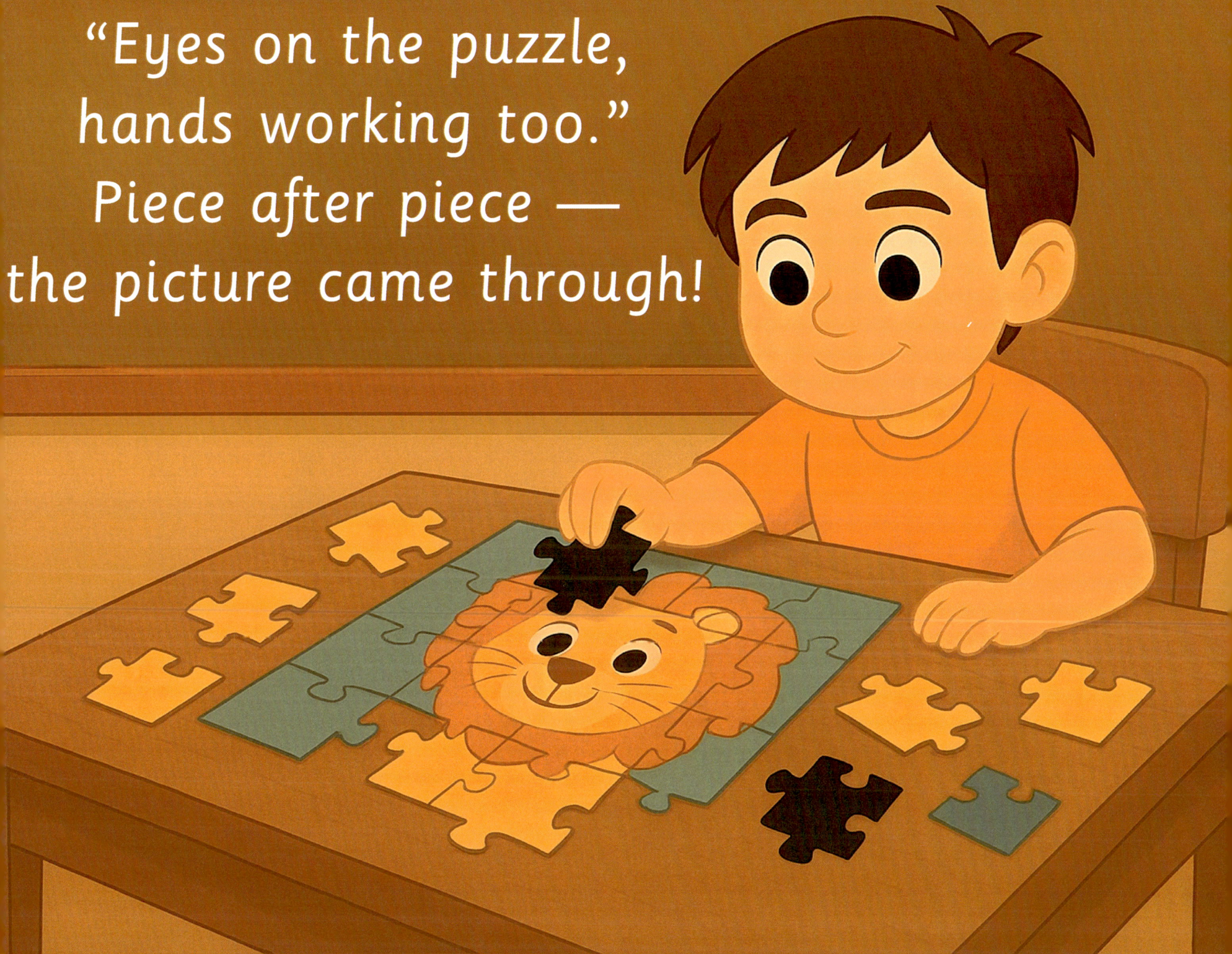

"Eyes on the puzzle,
hands working too."
Piece after piece —
the picture came through!

"Wow, Milo!" Emma clapped with cheer.
"Your focus made the lion appear!"

Now Emma's turn, she grinned so wide,
At martial arts class, the bag stood tall
with pride.

"Eyes on the bag, foot to the place!"
Kick — BOOM! She did it with power
and grace.

Her teacher smiled,
"That's focus, my dear.
With steady attention,
your strength will appear."

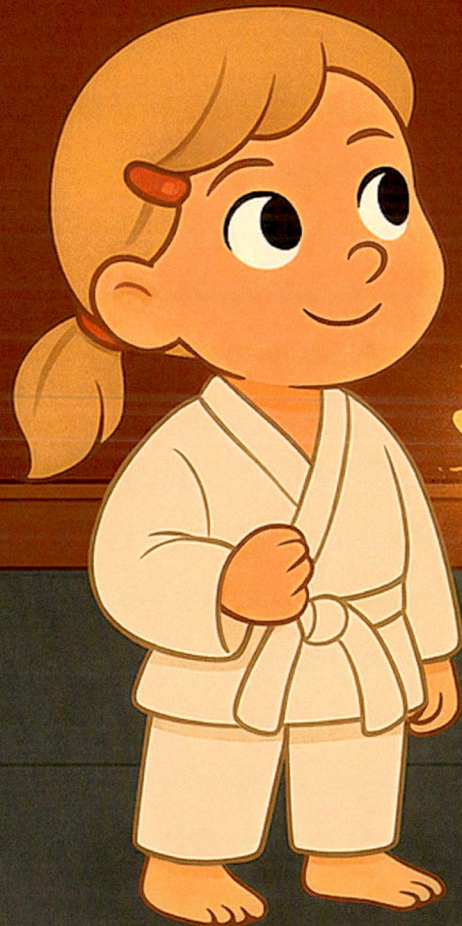

At home, the toys were scattered around.
Milo played cars, distractions abound.

But this time they said,
"Eyes on the toys."
We'll clean it up quick —
no fuss, just joys.

"Wow!" said Mom.
"You finished so fast!
That's the magic of focus —
it surely will last!"

Milo listened close,
with respect and a smile,
Waiting to answer and thinking
awhile.

Dad said with a smile,
"I'm proud of you two.
When you focus with care,
there's nothing you can't do."

Next day at school,
Milo raised his hand high.
He waited his turn,
not shouting out "Me!" or "I!"

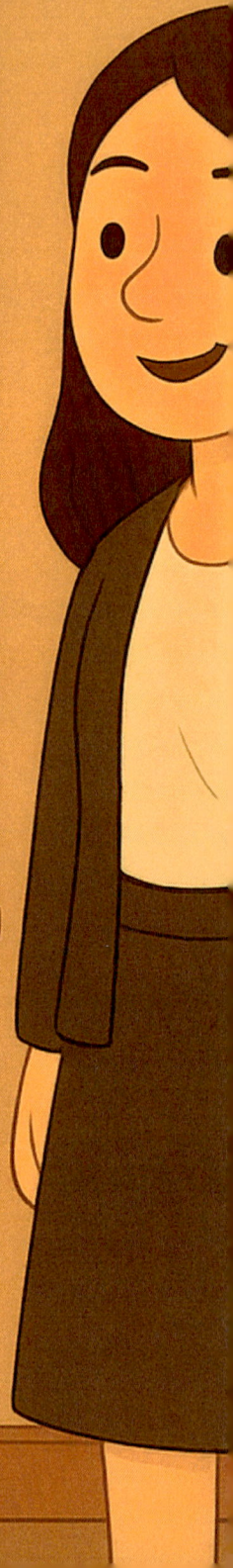

"Good job, Milo," the teacher smiled wide.
"Your focus will help you keep growing inside."

Later in practice, Emma stood tall.
She blocked and she punched —
the best of them all.

"Focus makes you strong and bright,
It helps you do each move just right."

On the playground, Milo wanted to climb.
He focused each step, one move at a time.

Emma pumped her legs on the swing.

Back and forth — what joy it did bring!

That night, Mom said with love in her eyes, "Focus helps you both to rise."

Dad hugged them close, his voice so kind, "Focus brings strength to body and mind."

At bedtime they whispered, tucked snug and tight,
"Focus brings growth, it makes us shine bright."

That night they dreamed, the stars in the sky.

With caps on their shoulders, they started to fly.

On each star, one word did gleam —
FOCUS! It shone like a powerful beam.

FOCUS

When morning arrived, they stretched with delight,

Brave, strong, and smart — their hearts felt so light.

At breakfast, Emma said with a grin,
"Focus is my superpower within!"

Now every time they hear the word,
They smile because their hearts are stirred.

Dear Parents,

Take this gift to heart,

Focus is strength — a wonderful start.

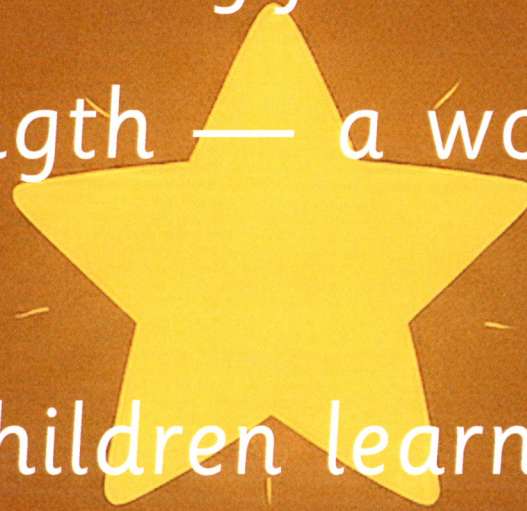

When children learn to give

tasks their care,

They shine at school,

at home, everywhere.

www.ingramcontent.com/pod-product-compliance
Lightning Source LLC
Chambersburg PA
CBRC102119040426
42452CB00005B/165